KAREN LATCHANA KENNEY

THE SCIENCE OF MUSIC

DISCOVERING SOUND

Checkerboard
Library

abdopublishing.com

Published by Abdo Publishing, a division of ABDO, PO Box 398166, Minneapolis, Minnesota 55439. Copyright © 2016 by Abdo Consulting Group, Inc. International copyrights reserved in all countries. No part of this book may be reproduced in any form without written permission from the publisher. Checkerboard Library™ is a trademark and logo of Abdo Publishing.

Printed in the United States of America, North Mankato, Minnesota

102015
012016

Design: Christa Schneider
Production: Mighty Media, Inc.
Editor: Rebecca Felix

Cover Photos: Shutterstock, front cover, back cover
Interior Photos: iStockphoto, pp. 23, 27; Mighty Media, Inc., pp. 4–5, 7, 11, 15, 17, 20; Shutterstock, 6, 8, 9, 11, 13, 14, 16, 17, 18, 19, 21, 25, 26, 28–29

Library of Congress Cataloging-in-Publication Data

Kenney, Karen Latchana, author.
  The science of music : discovering sound / by Karen Latchana Kenney.
     pages cm. -- (Science in action)
  Includes index.
  ISBN 978-1-62403-962-1
1. Sound--Juvenile literature. 2. Music--Acoustics and physics--Juvenile literature. 3. Musical instruments--Juvenile literature. I. Title.
  QC225.5.K376 2016
  534--dc23
                    2015026211

CONTENTS

FEEL THE BASS!

It's nice and quiet. You're about to write a paper for school. But your brother has different plans. He cranks up the stereo in his room. The music **radiates** through closed doors and solid walls. But the **vocals** are hard to hear. You can't quite make out what song it is.

4

Then the **bass** kicks in. You not only hear it, but you can also feel the sound. The windows rattle. Hanging pictures jiggle a little. Even your chest buzzes with the bass. It makes it hard to concentrate on homework!

What you hear, feel, and see comes from vibrating sound waves. These waves travel from the stereo through your house. The high notes move in shorter waves. They can't travel as far.

However, low bass notes have much longer waves. These waves move through thick objects, such as walls. As sound waves pass through matter, they make objects vibrate. The louder the sound, the more movement the waves create.

WHAT IS SOUND?

CHAPTER 1

A book makes no sound, right?
This is true when it is lying still,
but open it up. Turn the pages.
Listen as your fingers slide across
the paper. The sounds you hear
start with energy provided by you.

Sound is a form of energy transmitted in waves that are received by hearing.

All sounds require energy to
occur. This energy comes from a
source that creates a vibration.
This source may be a clap or loud bark. The created
vibration moves in waves away from the source through
a **medium**, such as air. The waves make the medium
vibrate as well.

Finally, the vibrations reach your ears. There, the
sound's energy is changed into messages. The messages
are sent to the brain, and you **perceive** them as sound.

MEASURING SOUND

A sound's loudness is measured in decibels (dB). A dB tells you how much force a sound wave carries. This is the sound's **amplitude**, or intensity.

Quiet sounds are lower on the dB scale. Louder sounds rank higher on the scale. Here is a chart of the dB levels of some everyday sounds. Sounds louder than 85 dB can damage human ears.

- 85 dB — BUSY CITY TRAFFIC
- 75 — WASHING MACHINE
- 65 — TYPICAL SPEECH
- 55 — RAINFALL
- 45
- 35
- 25 — WHISPER
- 15
- 5
- 0 dB — SOFTEST SOUND HUMANS CAN HEAR

7

WHAT IS MUSIC?

Listen to a crowded room at a party. People are talking, laughing, and moving. As you listen, you hear many sounds at once. Music also consists of many sounds at once. But the party sounds do not sound like music, do they? What's the difference?

The difference is that people arrange sounds to make music. Notes are combined to create a **unified** sound. The sounds from a party are not unified or arranged. They are **random**. So they are not music, correct? Well, not everyone agrees on what is musical.

To some people, jazz music is just noise. But to others it's a beautiful work of musical art. For that reason, music can be difficult to **define**. It can be different for everyone.

Music is the different arrangement of notes within scales.

People may interpret music differently, but they often bond over it too!

People often feel emotions when listening to music. Sometimes listeners feel happier after listening to a certain song. Or maybe music makes them feel relaxed. For others, music communicates a message.

Music is so important to people, it was sent as a message on a spacecraft launched in 1977. A record inside the spacecraft contains some songs from Earth. Humans hope that if aliens find the record, they may be able to understand something about us through our music.

TRAVELING WAVES

Have you ever been to a rock concert? Up close to the stage, the music is super loud. But back behind a large crowd, the music dies down. The farther you go from the stage, the quieter the music gets. Why is that? It has to do with the way sound travels from its source.

Sound energy waves have high and low points. The waves move away from their source at a certain speed. And to be heard, these waves must move through a **medium** made of matter. Different mediums affect a sound's volume.

All mediums are made of molecules. When vibrating sound waves enter the medium, they make these molecules vibrate as well. The vibrating molecules bouncing off one another use up some of the sound wave's energy. The vibrations spread outward, but there is less energy to push molecules as they do.

Invisible air molecules absorb some energy from traveling sound waves at a concert before they reach the audience's ears.

This causes the sound to become more and more quiet. So the farther you are from a source, the quieter the sound will be.

What if sound moved through something without molecules, such as a vacuum in space? There would be no sound at all. Sound waves cannot travel without molecules to move the vibrating sound waves along.

BOUNCING WAVES

Although sound moves through matter, there isn't always a clear path for its waves to travel through. Sometimes a sound wave can't move through something, so it bounces. When that happens, the sound reflects away from the object.

For example, try singing in an empty gym. You hear your voice make the sound. Then you hear the sound again within seconds. The sound waves bounced off the gym's walls. The waves reflected off the walls and traveled back toward you, so you heard the sound again. This is called an echo.

Scientists use echoes to find objects in hard-to-see places. They use technology to send a sound out and then listen for its echo. The time it takes for an echo to bounce off an object and travel back to the source can tell the object's location, size, and shape. This process is called echolocation.

Certain animals, such as bats, naturally have the ability to use echolocation. And some blind people have

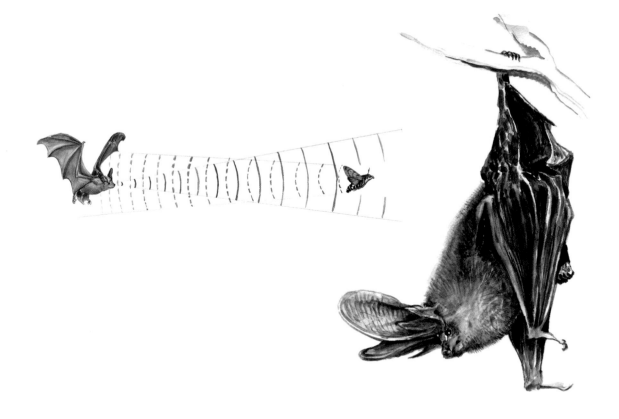

Bats use echolocation to track insects when hunting.

learned to use it to help them get around in the world.
These people send out voice clicks and listen for echoes
to determine how far away something is.

   Daniel Kish has been blind since the age of one. Kish
rides bikes and climbs mountains using echolocation. He
can determine different types of objects' locations by
how an echo sounds. The human brain also **perceives**
other sound properties, such as pitch and volume.

SOUND WAVE PATTERNS

The volume and pitch of sounds we hear has to do with the sound wave's properties. How loud or quiet a sound is depends on the wave's **amplitude**. This is measure of how much energy a sound wave has. It is seen as how high or low a sound wave **fluctuates** from a center point on the wave.

Amplitude is measured in dB. The higher a wave fluctuates from the wave's center point, the higher the amplitude, and the louder the sound.

Wavelength is another property of sound. Wavelength is a measure from one wave's high point to the next. How many wavelengths pass in a certain amount of time is a sound's **frequency**.

Dogs are able to hear a much higher frequency of sounds than people can.

Frequency is measured in hertz (Hz). A lower Hz means the sound wave has a longer wavelength. A higher Hz means a sound has a shorter wavelength. We hear frequency as a sound's pitch. This is how high or low a sound seems. A dog's growl has a low pitch, while a bird's screech has a much higher pitch.

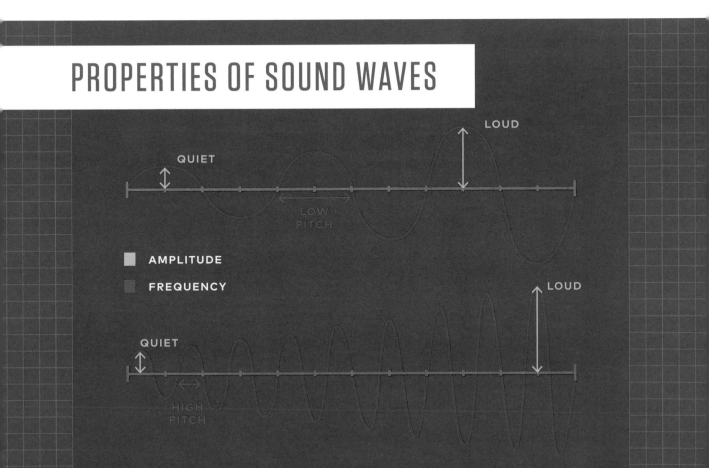

PROPERTIES OF SOUND WAVES

QUIET

LOUD

LOW PITCH

■ AMPLITUDE
■ FREQUENCY

QUIET

LOUD

HIGH PITCH

HEARING SOUND

The human ear is a **complex** organ that changes sound waves into messages our brains can understand. The part that sits on the surface of your head is your outer ear. You have a middle and inner ear as well.

Your outer ear directs sound waves into your ear canal. The vibrations travel through the canal's tube, where it meets the eardrum. This membrane vibrates

Tiny hairs are found deep within human ears. Without these hairs, we would not hear!

at the same **frequency** as the sound. The vibrations are then passed onto three bones in the middle ear. These bones are the malleus, incus, and stapes.

Next, the vibrations enter the cochlea. It holds fluid and special hair cells. When the vibrations hit the cochlea, the fluid and hair cells inside move too. They send electrical signals to the auditory nerve. The auditory nerve sends the signals to the brain, which interprets them as sounds.

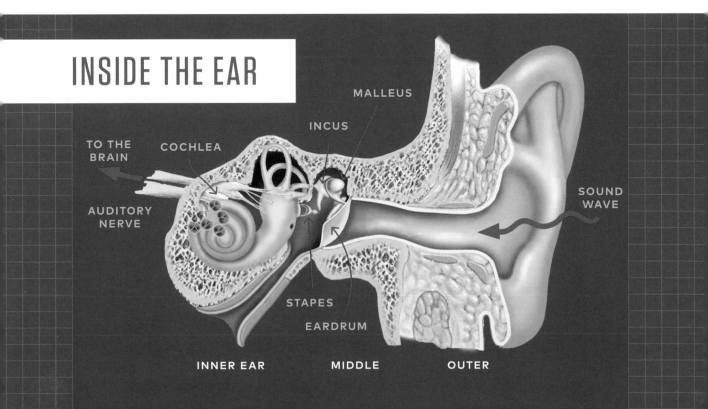

INSIDE THE EAR

MALLEUS

INCUS

TO THE BRAIN

COCHLEA

SOUND WAVE

AUDITORY NERVE

STAPES

EARDRUM

INNER EAR   MIDDLE   OUTER

DAMAGING SOUNDS

Human ears are able to hear a wide range of sounds, from whispers to loud rock concerts. But is that loud music okay for our ears? From a distance, far from the source of the sound, it may be. But the musicians onstage at a rock concert are right near the source, where the sound is very loud. Loud sounds can create hearing loss.

What these loud sounds do is damage the hair cells in the cochlea. Atop the hair cells are strands called stereocilia. When healthy, these strands stick straight up into the fluid and are able to detect its motion. If a loud sound damages them, the stereocilia bend over or break. Then the hair cell dies. It will never again send electric signals to the brain so it can **perceive** sound.

Being exposed to extremely loud sounds is the top cause of hearing loss in people.

18

The sound of fireworks exploding reaches around 145 dB, high within the range that can cause damage to human ears.

Just how loud are the sounds that cause this? Sounds above 85 dB can damage your ears. The sounds of a busy city street can reach near this level. The sounds a musician is exposed to in a rock concert can reach 110 dB. Professional musicians are four times more likely to have hearing loss due to very loud sounds. The length of their exposure influences this too.

The higher the dB level, the faster a sound can damage the ear. A 115 dB sound can take less than 30 seconds to cause damage. In addition to rock concerts, many other everyday sounds are louder than this. An ambulance siren is about 125 dB. And a gunshot can be 165 dB!

MAKING MUSIC

Loud or quiet, high or low, musical notes sound much different to us than other noises. This is because music sound waves create a melody, harmony, and rhythm. A noise is a **random** combination of sound vibrations.

Closing and locking a door is an example of a noise. The sound it makes is created from the door moving, the hinge sliding, the wall reacting, and the lock turning. The noises each action makes combine. But the noises are not related. So, their combined sound waves do not form a regular pattern.

The repeating sound wave pattern of a musical note versus the random sound waves of a noise

MUSICAL NOTE   NOISE

Musicians read and play the same musical notes on different instruments, creating a unified sound.

In contrast, a musical note's sound wave has a repeating pattern. This pattern repeats at 20 to 20,000 times per second in air. The human ear cannot hear any notes outside of that range.

Music is made up of a **succession** of notes with different pitches. The notes made by an instrument are named from the first seven letters of the alphabet, from A to G. Notes can also be flat or sharp, meaning they fall between the main seven pitches.

Musicians playing together tune their instruments to the same pitch. Then the sound waves of the notes in the music they play blend together. Different instruments play the same notes, creating the sounds in different ways.

INSTRUMENTAL VIBRATIONS

Because sound is made of vibrations, musical instruments must have vibrating systems to play notes. Many instruments, such as the flute, have long tubes for their vibrating systems. A player pushes air into the flute at one end. The air moves through the tube. Its molecules vibrate in a repeating wave, making a note. The player covers holes atop the flute to release the air at different places, creating different notes.

Stringed instruments, such as an **acoustic** guitar, make notes differently. Thick and thin strings stretch across a guitar's hollow body. Tightening or loosening the strings affects the guitar's sound. Tighter, thinner strings create higher pitches. Looser, thicker strings create lower pitches.

A player plucking a string creates a vibration that moves through the string. Plucking different strings creates different notes. The guitar's body vibrates too, which puts more air molecules in motion. This amplifies the sound inside the hollow space. Vibrations radiate from the guitar as notes.

LUDWIG VAN BEETHOVEN

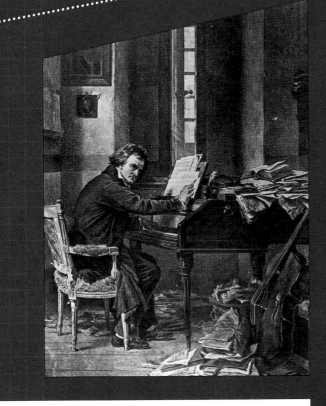

Classical music composer Ludwig van Beethoven was born in 1770 in Germany. He combined string and **vocal** music in new ways for the time. He wrote many famous works, of which many are still played today.

Around 1800, Beethoven began losing his hearing. In 1819, the composer was completely deaf. Despite his deafness, Beethoven continued composing music, writing some of his most **complex** works yet. He sawed off the legs of his piano so it touched the floor. This allowed its sounds to create vibrations in the floor. Beethoven could sit on the floor and play the piano by feeling its vibrations. He died in 1827, but Beethoven's music lives on through modern orchestras around the world.

Ludwig van Beethoven created more than 600 compositions in his life, beginning at the age of 12.

ROOM ACOUSTICS

Musicians practice their instruments for months before a concert. But do you know what can ruin their hard work? Playing in a room with bad **acoustics**.

The way a room is built affects how sound travels in it. For example, large pillars can break apart the sounds of music. A flat floor can stop musical vibrations from reaching an audience at the rear of a room. The vibrations get absorbed into the floor before they can reach this part of the room. And flat walls can reflect sound waves back and forth in a room, creating single reflections of sounds, or echoes.

Sound that **reverberates** is best for hearing music. This happens when a series of multiple sounds are directed to specific areas of a room. Designers build music auditoriums to achieve this kind of sound. Ceiling and wall panels positioned at different angles absorb and reflect sounds in specific directions. Carpet covers the floor, balcony fronts, and curved or flat surfaces. This helps absorb sounds where desired, and stop

Curved walls and domes, such as those in Radio City Music Hall in New York, can distribute reverberant sound.

echoes. Lastly, floors slope upward toward the rear. This helps sound travel to that part of the room.

A good **acoustic** design is important. It makes music sound full, rich, and clear throughout an auditorium. The audience hears the sounds of music at its best!

GOOD VIBRATIONS

Listen to the world around you. You'll hear sounds of all kinds, from the background noise of a busy street to the notes of a bird's song. The air is filled with the vibrations of sound waves.

Your ears are constantly receiving sound waves, even when you sleep! When you are awake, the brain

The world is full of sounds! Stop and listen wherever you are. What do you hear?

Making music using instruments can bring joy to you and those around you!

recognizes these waves as noises and sounds. Some vibrations repeat or are arranged in a certain way to make music. These sounds affect people in many ways.

Music makes some people want to move. They tap their feet, clap their hands, and dance. People also respond to music in emotional and physical ways. Music can lessen our stress and anxiety. The way music affects us is just one part of what makes sound, and the way we hear it, so amazing!

SEEING VIBRATIONS

AN EXPERIMENT WITH SOUND WAVES

EXPERIMENT

QUESTION

Can you create visible sound vibrations at home?

RESEARCH

You've already learned that sounds are vibrations moving through different **mediums** (see page 5). Can you make visible sound vibrations at home? Here are some materials you will need to find out:

- radio or stereo
- speakers
- glass bowl
- water
- earplugs (optional)

PREDICT

What will happen when you place a bowl of water on a speaker and then turn up the volume? **Predict** what will happen. Write it down.

TEST

1. Fill the bowl with water. Set on a table close to the speakers.

2. Turn on the radio or stereo. Play a song that you like.

3. Set the volume as loud as you are allowed. Ask a parent first! You may also want to put earplugs in your ears.

4. Watch the water in the bowl, especially when the song's **bass** becomes loud. What does the water do?

ASSESS

Was your prediction correct? Did the water move? Why or why not? Write down your thoughts. Did any other objects nearby vibrate too? Turn up the volume again and find out!

GLOSSARY

acoustic – a musical instrument whose sound is created using its body shape and is not dependent on electrical equipment.

acoustics – properties of a room that affect how sound waves bounce and how sounds are heard.

amplitude – maximum height of a sound wave from its middle point.

bass – having a low sound or pitch.

complex – having many parts, details, ideas, or functions.

define – to describe or explain something.

fluctuate – to keep changing back and forth or up and down.

frequency – the number of waves, such as sound waves, passing a fixed point each second.

medium – a substance through which something passes through or is carried, such as air.

perceive – to use the sense to become aware of something.

predict – to guess something ahead of time on the basis of observation, experience, or reasoning.

radiate – to move outward from the center.

random – lacking a definite plan or pattern.

reverberate – to continue in a series of quickly repeated sounds that bounce off a surface such as a wall.

succession – things that follow one another in order.

unify – to bring together or make into one.

vocal – related to the voice.

WEBSITES

To learn more about Science in Action, visit **booklinks.abdopublishing.com.** These links are routinely monitored and updated to provide the most current information available.

INDEX